AMERICA...
LEG...

Proposals for Ranking
the   of
Gove   ams

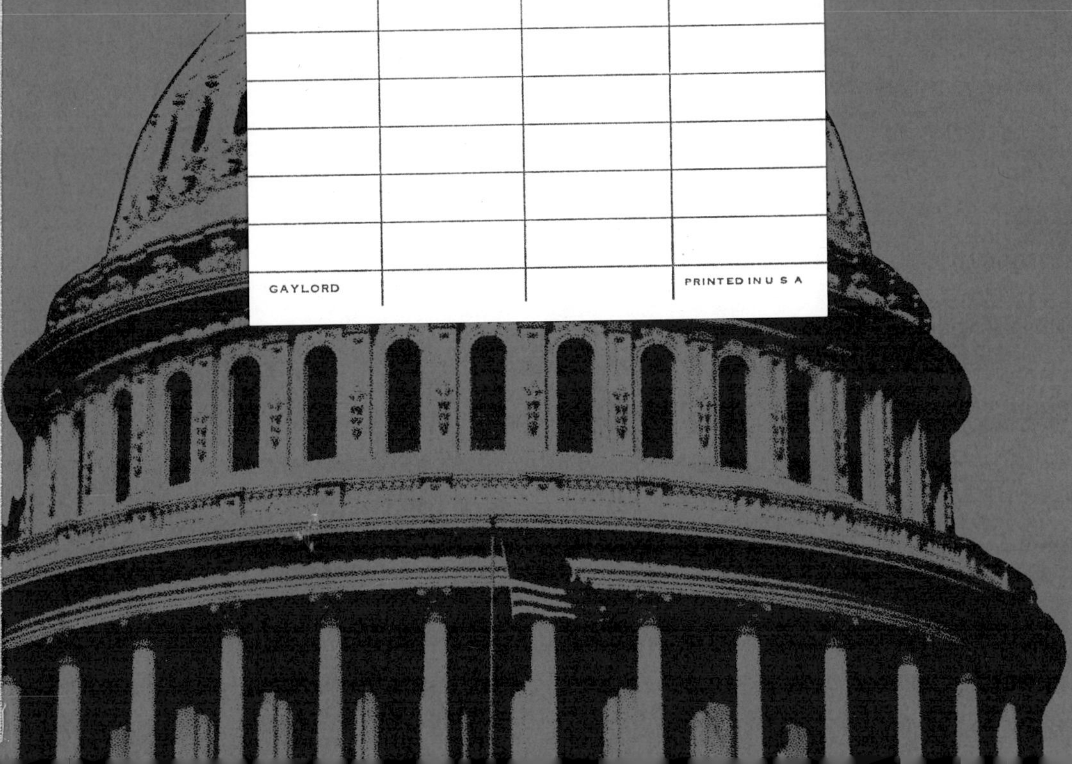

AEI LEGISLATIVE ANALYSES
Balanced analyses of current proposals before the Congress, prepared with the help of specialists in law, economics, and government

Proposals for Ranking the Effectiveness of Government Programs

1980
96th Congress
2nd Session

AMERICAN ENTERPRISE INSTITUTE
for Public Policy Research
Washington, D.C.

ISBN 0-8447-0229-3
Legislative Analysis No. 14, 96th Congress
February 1980

Contents

1

Introduction

Politicians and policy analysts have long been frustrated over the difficulty of cutting or eliminating government programs. Every program immediately acquires a constituency among certain voters and within the bureaucracy, and these groups can muster powerful, and usually effective, opposition whenever "their" programs are threatened with termination or a reduction in funding.

Many believe that the power of such special interest groups can be limited if the Congress and the executive branch intensify their oversight procedures and periodically ask which programs are effectively accomplishing their goals and which are not. Oversight is often pushed aside by current crises, however, and there seems to be a higher political reward for new program creation than for effective oversight. It is widely believed, therefore, that oversight and program evaluation procedures will not be successful unless the Congress and the executive branch create a rigid schedule which imposes a strict discipline on the process.

Many presidents and congressmen have struggled with the problem of devising efficient procedures which would impose such discipline. President Johnson attempted to implement a Planning, Programming, and Budgeting System (PPBS). PPBS is a program-oriented (as opposed to an organization-oriented) management approach which examines needs over the long run and evaluates programs having similar objectives accordingly. It worked with some success in the early 1960s within the Defense Department, but when applied throughout the executive branch it proved to be too arduous and did not long survive the Johnson presidency.

More recently, President Carter implemented Zero Base Budgeting (ZBB) to provoke more intensive policy evaluation within the executive branch. Congress also is considering sunset laws, which would automatically terminate programs according to a rigid schedule unless Congress explicitly votes for new budget authority following program reexamination. ZBB and sunset laws were described in detail and evaluated in a 1978 legislative analysis.[1]

A relatively new proposal, which would complement such procedures by spotlighting particularly ineffective programs, is the Government Accountability Act. This analysis will examine the terms of that proposal and the principal arguments for and against its enactment.

2

BACKGROUND

The impetus for devising means for eliminating certain government programs, or at a minimum targeting certain programs for measures that will improve their efficiency and effectiveness, stems from increasing public and congressional awareness of certain realities. Congress finds it increasingly difficult to fund new government programs and to continue funding for old programs that rarely are terminated, without voting for unpopular and burdensome new taxes or allowing inflation to raise average tax rates. (Allowing the current inflation rate to raise average tax rates provides all of the increases that would ever be needed.) Tax revenues available to fund government programs are finite, but demands for government spending are infinite.[2] Congress, it is claimed, is less and less able to eliminate unneeded or ineffective government programs on an ad hoc basis, because Congress is more and more removed from the results of its legislative work. The Senate Committee on Governmental Affairs attributes this removal to the vast number and complexity of government programs, the dramatic increase in the percentage of the federal budget devoted to so-called uncontrollable expenditures, and the even more rapid growth in the cost of federal programs with permanent appropriations.[3] The dilemma that policy makers face is reflected in a statement supporting sunset legislation made by President Carter:

> Too many federal programs have been enacted and then allowed to
> continue indefinitely, without further thought. The country's needs
> and priorities change, and we must assure that government pro-
> grams change with them.[4]

As Senator Edmund S. Muskie (D-Me.) put it, "we . . . are increasingly unable to do an effective job of legislating for the future because our hands are so bound by the past."[5] The growth of so-called uncontrollable expenditures is putting pressure on expenditures for controllable items and reducing the policy options available to the Congress in determining priorities for federal spending.[6]

Impetus for reform also stems from the public perception that many government programs duplicate or overlap other government programs. Senator Joseph R. Biden, Jr. (D-Del.) argued in favor of sunset legislation that in 1976 there were 1,030 domestic assistance programs administered by 52 federal agencies for the benefit of the 50 states and 80,000 units of local government. He noted that there are 302 different programs administered by 11 separate federal agencies in the health field alone, and there are 259 programs in the area of community development.[7] Senator Muskie stated that we have made little progress in streamlining and simplifying the many programs on the books, and we still have overlapping programs scattered all over downtown and Capitol Hill.[8] (Some observers feel that sunset and related measures will not work because Congress and the administration cannot deal seriously with so many programs in the time required.) Highly vocal special interest groups have succeeded in preserving existing programs from termination, budget cuts, or reform in most instances, even though a majority of the voters favor reducing government expenditures and eliminating inefficient and overlapping programs. The wrath of the general public has not been targeted on specific programs and has been too diffuse to offset the pressures of these special interest groups. The result, critics contend, is the unspoken rule that money spent on a program in one year must be continued or increased in the following year.[9]

Additional impetus for reform stems from the congressional and public perception that government programs are plagued by widespread fraud and mismanagement. Senator Charles H. Percy (R-Ill.) cites the estimate of the Senate Governmental Affairs Committee that General Services Administration employees stole $66 million a year from the government. GSA losses may amount to $100 million a year, according to some estimates, when noncriminal negligence is taken into account. Senator Muskie contends that many government programs entail huge expenditures for administrative costs and overhead and that grant programs such as water supply research grants involve administrative costs of 28 percent.[10] Senator Percy contends that one reason taxpayers are justifiably angered over the growth in government spending is government's seeming inability to improve or eliminate programs not meeting their promised objectives.[11]

Senator Muskie argues that new government programs can be financed in one of only four ways: by running massive deficits and sending inflation through the roof; by raising taxes substantially to pay for new programs; by across-the-board cuts in spending; or by selective cuts in existing programs that may no longer be necessary. He argues the first two of these options would be both economic and political suicide; the third option would make room in the budget for new programs, but it would do so in an irresponsible and indiscriminate manner; and the final option, while the most difficult, would be the most responsible of the four.[12]

There is still another source for the impetus to cut specific government programs on a selective basis. The late Representative William A. Steiger (R-Wis.) argued for adoption of a mechanism for cutting selected government programs in order to make room for federal tax cuts.[13]

The Government Accountability Act was originally conceived by former Ambassador Laurence H. Silberman "to help identify those relatively ineffective government programs eligible for termination."[14] A system of ranking programs by agency would show up relatively ineffective government programs as candidates for elimination or improvement, thus allowing for easier and better management of the federal government.

Senator Percy and Representative Steiger incorporated Silberman's proposals into the Government Accountability Act of 1978, which was introduced in August 1978. Since the bill was introduced late in the session, little action was taken on it. When S.2—the Sunset Act of 1978—came up for debate on the floor of the Senate, however, Senator Percy offered an amendment which made the Government Accountability Act a separate title of S.2. The amendment was passed by the Senate, as was S.2, but no floor action was taken on the Sunset Act of 1978 in the House of Representatives, and the bill died with the adjournment of the 95th Congress.

In the 96th Congress the Government Accountability Act was reintroduced in both the House and the Senate. Senators Percy and Carl Levin (D-Mich.) introduced the bill in the Senate (S.1161), while Representative Gerald B. H. Solomon (R-N.Y.) introduced it as H.R. 755, Representative Edwin B. Forsythe (R-N.J.) introduced it as H.R. 1944, and Representatives John N. Erlenborn (R-Ill.), Richard A. Gephardt (D-Mo.), Don Fuqua (D-Fla.), and Frank Horton (R-N.Y.) introduced it as H.R. 4114. The Sunset Act was reintroduced in the Senate (S.2) by Senator Muskie and 62 cosponsors and in the House (H.R. 2) by Representatives James J. Blanchard (D-Mich.), Norman Y. Mineta (D-Calif.), and Gephardt with 162 cosponsors in the form that it passed the Senate, thus including the Government Accountability Title (Title VI).

Most of the action on the Government Accountability Act has involved its consideration as a title of the Sunset Act. Discussion of the Government Accountability title during hearings held on sunset before the Senate Committee on Governmental Affairs led to one day of testimony that dealt solely with that title. Limited discussion of the title occurred in the House during sunset hearings held before subcommittees of the Committee on Governmental Operations and the Committee on Rules.

3

THE GOVERNMENT ACCOUNTABILITY ACT

The Government Accountability Act would require the President to submit a management report to Congress at the beginning of each Congress along with his budget message. In the management report the President would rank all programs within each executive department and independent establishment ("independent establishment" includes the U.S. Postal Service and the Postal Rate Commission, but does not include the General Accounting Office or the independent regulatory agencies). The programs are to be ranked as to their effectiveness relative to all other programs within that department or independent establishment. The President is also to grade each of the programs on its relative effectiveness as "excellent," "adequate," or "unsatisfactory." The ranking and grading of programs is to be determined by three criteria:

- the clarity of the law and the statutory objective upon which the program is based
- the overall implementation of the program by the responsible executive department or independent establishment
- the overall quality of the management of the program by the responsible executive department or independent establishment.[15]

The President is also to include reasons for his evaluations, and recommendations for administrative or legislative improvements.

Under the bill, the director of the Office of Management and Budget is to submit a report to the President evaluating federal programs. This report is to be forwarded by the President to the Congress as part of the management report. The director of OMB is to identify any programs, including those of the independent regulatory agencies, that are contradictory to other federal programs, and he must suggest legislation to terminate or modify programs whose relative ineffectiveness no longer justifies continued federal expenditures or justifies a lower level of expenditures. S. 2 and H.R. 2 omit the affirmative requirement that the director identify contradictory programs carried out by independent regulatory agencies.[16]

The President is also to include in the management report his recommendations and proposals in regard to the director's report. Supplementary reports to the management report may be submitted to the Congress by the President in the interim between his biennial reports if he feels such supplementary or revised recommendations are needed. The director of OMB is also authorized to submit supplementary reports to the President.

4

ARGUMENTS IN FAVOR OF THE GOVERNMENT ACCOUNTABILITY ACT

BENEFITS OF RANKING PROGRAM EFFECTIVENESS

Identifying Ineffective Programs. The authors of the Government Accountability Act believe that:

> The public confidence in the ability of the Congress and the executive branch to manage the federal government effectively has declined.

> The federal government is not as accountable as it should be in serving the public interest.[17]

Proponents of the bill feel that the procedure of ranking federal programs established by the bill will correct this situation. Statements by the coauthors of the legislation stress this belief.

> The goal of our bill is quite simple. Namely, to provide the public and Congress with a ranking of federal programs so that those glaringly ineffective and mismanaged programs will stand out.[18]

> What the rankings will mean is that Congress can get a better handle on determining which federal programs could be improved or weeded out and which deserve more or less money than they're currently being given. They will also allow us to deal with the problems of overlapping or of contrasting goals.[19]

According to proponents, the ranking of programs as to effectiveness constitutes a mechanism that would counter the information provided by the program's constituents, who obviously want the program to survive. Any program that repeatedly appears at the bottom of the rankings would clearly be ineffective, wasteful, and thus expendable. It is only these expendable programs that would be proposed for elimination, while other low ranking ones would be clearly seen as candidates for improvements. Conversely, programs that repeatedly appear at the top of the list would be examined to find the reasons for their effectiveness and efficiency.

Proponents argue that:

> Although this measure will not solve all the problems related to Government spending or eliminating those programs which have simply outlived their usefulness, it will give us the assessment tool we so sorely need.[20]

In sum, proponents believe the Government Accountability Act would increase accountability for the effectiveness or ineffectiveness of government programs. If ineffective programs are weeded out or improved, the public's perception of the ability of the executive branch to manage would improve.

Introducing Competition into Government Operations. Section 2(a) of the bill states:

> The Federal Government, unlike private enterprise, has no built-in mechanism for calling attention to and eliminating programs that are not proving to be cost effective.

As Senator Percy has argued:

> In private industry the waste and corruption we have seen in several Federal agencies would not go undetected for long. Businesses have too much to lose to tolerate this kind of inefficiency and intrigue. Those that do not police their own ranks are soon out of business or before the bankruptcy judge.[21]

In other words, a business must remain efficient and competitive to survive, but no such pressure is now felt by government agencies.

Proponents of the bill realize that it is not possible to introduce the same intense competition found in private markets into government operations and that there is "a long way to go in even trying to bring a semblance of efficiency into Federal program management."[22] The bill would introduce some competition into the public sector because it "would induce Americans to think of government programs as competing against each other for limited resources."[23] The ranking of programs would show what programs deserve a higher priority in competition for scarce funding and would best use these limited resources. Since programs with low rankings would run the risk of elimination, their managers would have an incentive to improve their particular programs or risk loss of financing.

Providing Incentives for Better Management. Not only is it held that this act would increase competition between managers of departmental programs, it is also argued that it would introduce a new form of competition; it would provide better, rather than just larger, government programs. Proponents feel that the present political environment in which managers operate is not conducive to better management of programs because there is no qualitative competition.

Currently, cabinet and subcabinet officers have an incentive to devote most of their time and energy in their relatively short stay in an agency to expanding their empires by creating new programs. There is no incentive to expend their resources on better management of existing programs because such efforts are often overlooked and unrewarded. An appointee gains the most attention and political benefits by launching ambitious new programs, which produce even more attention and benefits when accomplished by legislation. These efforts receive the most press coverage and publicity because it appears that something is being done about perceived problems.

It is not only the person who expands programs and departments (rather than opting for better management of existing programs) who receives more recognition—and the political gains that follow; appointees who are marked as good managers are often esteemed for the wrong reasons. "Too often, the press naively labels those appointees who have minimal management impact on their agencies and consequently do not attract internal criticism as the good managers."[24]

Proponents believe the management report—particularly the ranking of programs—would remedy the problem.

> The Management Report will serve notice to agency executives that their tenure will be evaluated not only by their new program initiatives but, more importantly, by their success in administering existing programs.[25]

Managers would be "faced with a day of program reckoning" and thus induced to devote greater time and effort to managing their programs than to expanding them. Which appointee would want to see his programs at the bottom of his department's list, especially if this position represents a decline from the previous year? Also, a program judged ineffective and with a low ranking would not be a good prospect for expansion, so future expansion would be directly linked to current performance levels.

Effectiveness in Achieving the Bill's Objectives

Subdivision of Programs for Evaluation. Current oversight procedures may provide an incentive for department heads to lump programs together. This camouflages weak and inefficient programs with effective, efficient, and popular programs. (Some opponents of the act argue that the act will encourage this.)

Some believe that this act will induce the breakdown of an agency's activities into smaller measurable units. Inefficient programs would be separated from efficient ones, so that those programs that appear at the bottom of the department's ranking (which of course are the most vulnerable to elimination or cuts in funding) would be a lesser parcel of the departmental empire. Otherwise, popular and efficient programs would also face close examination and possible elimination or modification. In other words, instead of inefficient programs being kept afloat by stronger programs (as is currently the case), they would be cast on their own to prevent them from dragging down efficient programs.

Publicizing Effectiveness Rankings. Press coverage and public recognition are believed to influence the management decisions of cabinet and subcabinet officers. Proponents of the act also note that truly good managers often go unnoticed. Through public release of the management report, the act is supposed to make good and bad management—and those who accomplish it—more visible.

The public nature of the program ranking would permit the public to participate in the oversight process for the first time. Proponents of the bill deem this fact very important:

> The importance of public release of the rankings cannot be overstated. This will provide the opportunity for input by individuals and organizations affected by a particular program. By so doing, we provide a safeguard against an administration attempting to sabotage a program or agency for ideological reasons.[26]

Such public participation in the evaluation process would take the form of constituents of—and special interest groups directly affected by—a particular program, pressing that department for better management of the program to ensure its survival. Also, members of the House and Senate would receive pressure from their constituents to cut programs that are constantly appearing at the bottom of the rankings; resources released from the weak and inefficient programs would be considered available for use in more beneficial programs.

Proponents of the act contend that the public and the press will pick up on the management report and its rankings (opponents hold that this will be just another in an already too large set of presidential reports), because there are clearly identifiable "winners" and "losers." Such identification is viewed by some political analysts as the ingredient that commands the most attention in Washington, and thus the management report would not be ignored. It is also argued that the press likes to regard public affairs as sport, which the definition of winners and losers will allow the press to do. "The 'report card' might captivate a nation that is fond of lists and rankings, such as college football polls."[27]

Creating a Consensus. The act's sponsors believe that a uniform method of evaluating programs would make it easier to reach a political consensus on which programs are least effective and eligible for reform. Currently there is no such consensus, because present evaluations of government programs are complicated and confusing and attain little attention from the press.

SUPERIORITY OVER OTHER SPENDING CONTROL METHODS

Proponents of the Government Accountability Act contend that it will be more effective than other methods that have been proposed to control government spending. Across-the-board spending cuts are criticized as an indiscriminate approach that does not single out ineffective and inefficient programs for termination or reduction. Such an approach may cripple or shortchange the good programs along with the bad ones. A constitutional amendment to require a balanced budget or to limit spending to a percentage of some indicator such as gross national product suffers from the same vice, for it fails to deal with the hard question of ferreting out the programs that should be cut. The Government Accountability Act, on the other hand, directs its attention to just that question. In addition, proponents claim that it will identify programs that need improvement, and with improvement in such programs tax money can be used more effectively and efficiently.

While the Government Accountability Act complements sunset and ZBB proposals, proponents of the act contend that sunset and ZBB are not an adequate substitute for it. Thus they note Senator Muskie's admission that sunset, as proposed in the Senate in 1978, calls for reconsideration but not reevaluation of programs.[28] Proponents contend that the reevaluation called for by the Government Accountability Act is the critical need. ZBB is criticized for its failure to effect the termination of any significant number of programs or to effect great economies.[29] Proponents contend that congressional budget procedures are no substitute for the Government Accountability Act. Thus, the congressional budget process sets an overall target for expenditures without coming to grips with the performance of agencies or the determination of which agencies should be abolished. Proponents contend the evaluative function that the Government Accountability Act would provide is missing from the congressional review of budget items.[30]

5

ARGUMENTS AGAINST THE GOVERNMENT ACCOUNTABILITY ACT

INADEQUATE SHOWING OF NEED

Critics of the Government Accountability Act contend that in many ways the information required by the proposal would duplicate that already sent to Congress or readily available to Congressional committees in connection with their oversight authority and under normal budget procedures. There would also be a duplication of each sunset review cycle if separate sunset legislation is enacted. The act's critics claim that the confidential information and rankings OMB now uses in formulating the President's budget are available to the relevant congressional committees on request and that no new law is needed to make that information available.

Critics note that ZBB has recently been introduced in the executive departments and agencies. As experience is gained with ZBB, they expect it to provide the procedures that will identify programs that should be terminated or reformed. That process involves administrators at all levels in rating activities and evaluating the cost effectiveness of old and new programs. ZBB will force agency heads and Congress to consider alternatives to existing programs for achieving their objectives. It will force a comparison of the efficiency and effectiveness of programs that seek to deal with the same objectives, while much of the comparison and ranking of programs under the Government Accountability Act will involve ranking of programs that do not have similar objectives, rather like comparing apples and oranges. Under ZBB no segment of the budget is sacred, not even so-called uncontrollable items. ZBB will force the identification of measurable objectives for programs and compel the qualitative and quantitative evaluation of accomplishments as they relate to long-run objectives.

Critics note that sunset, if enacted, will add another tool for dealing with inefficient and ineffective programs. Sunset, they claim, will shift the burden of proof from those who wish to terminate a program to those who wish to continue it. Systematic review of programs will replace the scattershot approach at oversight hearings. The most serious candidates for termination will be given the most thorough scrutiny. The relevant congressional committees will have the benefit of the impartial judgment of the General Accounting Office and as much information as they wish from the executive branch when review is undertaken.

Some critics of the bill argue that the management report is unnecessary. even without sunset and ZBB, in that the ranking and analysis of programs that it provides is also available in incremental budgeting. When there is a limited amount of money to be budgeted to an agency, the budget request of the agency's director will reflect his priority ranking and complete analysis of programs. Incremental budgeting does call for programs to be compared against each other with regard to efficiency, effectiveness, and importance. Programs given a high priority by the director will get a larger incremental request than those programs judged not so necessary, which obviously will have a smaller incremental request. In other words, inherent in the numbers of a budget is a ranking of programs by priority and effectiveness, and the management report would just duplicate this information.

Burden of Compliance

Critics of the Government Accountability Act argue that the bill places too much of a burden upon OMB, which estimates that there would be somewhere between 3,000 and 4,000 programs to be analyzed. Critics believe that OMB would produce a large part of the President's management report as well as the director's report, and this would be a major new undertaking for OMB. Compliance with the bill by OMB would "add substantially to OMB's and the agencies' workload, divert scarce resources, and complicate immensely the data management problems with the President's Budget."[31] Estimates of the size of the director's report, in which the programs included in the management report and those of the independent regulatory agencies are to be evaluated, are quite large. "It would take 3,000 pages, in our judgment, maybe twice that, to meet fully such requirements."[32]

Two other factors, critics argue, would contribute to making the burden and workload that the Government Accountability Act would place upon OMB larger than what is expected by the authors of the act. First, in preparing the director's report, OMB will not just be reformulating other rankings and reports it receives or produces, most specifically those that deal with ZBB. ZBB rankings and reports evaluate different decision packages, which reflect small changes in spending on different program combinations. A report and ranking on the effectiveness, productivity, and overlapping objectives of federal programs would require a very different analysis. Second, basically the same information and processes will be used to create both the President's and the director's part of the management report, and OMB will do much of the President's portion. Separating the management report into two distinct parts is seen by critics of the bill to be counterproductive and to create extra paperwork.

The additional workload created for OMB would occur simultaneously with final preparation of the President's budget. Presently, OMB is already operating at full capacity in the weeks prior to release of the President's budget, and it is expected that meeting the requirements of the Government Accountability Act would create serious problems. Bowman Cutter, executive associate director of OMB, noted: "In my judgment the combination of frequency, timing and immensity would simply preclude OMB at this point, given the resources it now has, from getting out a budget."[33]

The Government Accountability Act, critics feel, authorizes another in the series of unnecessary reports, and increases the paperwork burden that has plagued the legislative and executive branches in recent years at substantial cost to the taxpayers.

INEFFECTIVENESS IN ACHIEVING THE BILL'S OBJECTIVES

Distorting Rankings and Effectiveness Ratings. The process of ranking programs by relative effectiveness and grading their effectiveness is not immune from distortions. The rankings currently called for either formally by ZBB or informally by OMB are often not representative of real departmental priorities. Games are played with the rankings to prevent weak, inefficient, and unpopular programs from being cut, thus decreasing the size of the department head's empire.

One method used to defeat the purpose of current rankings is to rank programs in the reverse order of their popularity. The most politically popular programs are listed at the bottom, signifying that they are the most eligible for budget cuts, while unpopular programs are ranked at the top. Thus neither may be cut. Just as there is an incentive to play this game with current program rankings, there would also be benefits from this game with the ranking required by the Government Accountability Act.

Another game currently played with program rankings is to lump programs into larger groups for evaluation. This allows unpopular, ineffective, and inefficient programs to be camouflaged by popular, effective, and efficient programs. If press coverage and intraagency competition fails to prevent this method from being used—as critics of the bill argue—this aggregation of programs would also make it difficult to achieve the goals of the Government Accountability Act.

Lack of an Action-Forcing Mechanism. Critics argue that there is no action-forcing mechanism in the Government Accountability Act mandating or ensuring that Congress will act on the recommendations in the management report, even assuming the rankings and ratings in that report are accurate, which is by no means certain. Press coverage is likely to focus on a very few problems, and in any event press criticism of politically popular but largely ineffectual programs in the past has not caused their termination. There is no magic, it is claimed, in the submission of a mass of rankings and ratings on a firm schedule. Indeed, a new administration would not have sufficient time to review thousands of government programs and submit meaningful ratings and rankings at the same time as it must submit its first budget. Since Congress already has access to or can easily obtain ratings and rankings currently made within the executive branch, critics argue that not enough will be gained from the proposed new rankings to offset the burden and cost of the proposal.

Political Nature of Termination Process. Critics of the Government Accountability Act claim that it will be ineffective for yet another reason. They claim that termination of government programs is a political process and that termination rarely results from bureaucratic determinations or ratings. The programs that gain congressional acceptance when they are established generally have or develop strong constituencies. Termination of programs with other than weak constituencies is unlikely because members of Congress cannot ignore the political equation. Thus, bureaucratic rankings and ratings may have little to do with the continuation or funding of programs. The Law Enforcement Assistance Administration, critics say, has made little measurable progress toward achieving its objective of eradicating crime, but what member of Congress can vote to do nothing about crime? In sum, critics of the Government Accountability Act contend the management report is likely to become just another in a series of expensive and time-consuming reports that are prepared and then neglected.

6

The Compromise Proposal

During hearings on sunset laws before the Senate Governmental Affairs Committee, Bowman Cutter stated OMB's opposition to the Government Accountability Act title of S.2. Arguing that the burden would be too large and that the information supplied pursuant to the act would duplicate information already being transmitted to Congress, Cutter recommended deletion of the title. Senator Percy then requested meetings between his and Cutter's staffs to see if some compromise could be worked out that, while still retaining the essence of the original proposal, was satisfactory to OMB. These meetings were fruitful, producing changes that were acceptable to both delegations and directly addressing several of the arguments against the original proposal. The compromise title was proposed as a substitute and accepted during markup of S.2 by the Governmental Affairs Committee.

As modified, the Government Accountability Act title of S.2 would require the President to submit to Congress every two years an accountability report that assesses program effectiveness and also provides information that would assist Congress in program review and reauthorization. The accountability report would be submitted to Congress no later than May 1 of the first year of each Congress and should cover programs scheduled for reauthorization in accordance with the sunset reauthorization cycle established by S.2.

The accountability report would include a ranking of the effectiveness of programs within the same budget subfunction category. These program rankings are to be based on three criteria:

- the degree to which the program is achieving its statutory objectives
- the extent to which a program is counterproductive because of objectives that are in conflict with or duplicative of other programs in its subfunctional area
- the overall quality of the management of the program by the responsible executive department or independent establishment.[34]

The title also requires that the President include in the accountability report a brief explanation of his rankings and a list of those programs or areas the President recommends for termination or improvement.

Arguments for the Compromise Proposal

Proponents of the modified Government Accountability Act title of S.2 believe it is a workable and useful management tool for both the Congress and the executive branch. This is also the view of OMB:

With Title VI, we have a good opportunity to organize an evaluation effort at OMB that will be more effective and provide us with better results.[35]

Proponents of the compromise believe that it will correct major criticisms of the original government accountability title and make Congress and the executive branch more accountable to the public.

The burden the government accountability title would place on OMB would be reduced by elimination of the director's report and by tying its operation to the sunset reauthorization process. Since only one-fifth of all government programs would come up for sunset review in each Congress, requiring the accountability report to cover only those programs scheduled for sunset would cut the burden on OMB by four-fifths. Also, since the accountability report would be due on May 1 of the first year of each Congress, it would not interfere as much with OMB's preparation of the President's budget.

Tying the Government Accountability Act to the sunset process is also viewed as important because it provides an action-forcing mechanism. Proponents claim that this will ensure that the accountability report will not become just another unnecessary presidential report. The accountability report will provide important information about those programs specifically under review in that Congress and will thus be very valuable to those conducting the review.

ARGUMENTS AGAINST THE COMPROMISE PROPOSAL

Critics of the compromise proposal contend that it will not require the reporting of serious flaws in statutory or agency design of programs or the lack of statutory clarity even though these may be major reasons why a program is not performing well. Moreover, comparison in the rankings would be limited to other programs in the same budget subfunctional area, but this may not reveal much, for all such programs may be performing poorly or at about the same level. In addition, the rating for a particular program will be given only once every ten years. Since many programs involving the expenditure of large sums of money will not be included in the sunset review cycle, these programs will escape the accountability review entirely. The ten-year cycle of review for the remaining programs will give administrators ample opportunity to decide on the bureaucratic games they wish to employ to preserve particular programs that might otherwise be prime candidates for extinction. In sum, critics see the compromise as a less effective alternative. In addition, some critics feel that paperwork requirements would still be enormous and that this alternative may provide more information than can be dealt with effectively by decision makers.

Notes to Text

[1] *Zero-Base Budgeting and Sunset Legislation* (Washington, D.C.: American Enterprise Institute, 1978).

[2] *Congressional Record,* vol. 125 (May 16, 1979), p. S 6090, statement of Senator Charles H. Percy (R-Ill.).

[3] Senate Report 95-326, p. 3.

[4] *Congressional Record,* vol. 124 (October 11, 1978), p. S 18187.

[5] Ibid., p. S 18167.

[6] Ibid., p. S 18194, statement of Senator Joseph R. Biden, Jr. (D-Del.).

[7] Ibid., pp. S 18193-S 18194, statement of Senator Biden. Senator Biden also referred to the Senate Government Operations Committee's finding that there were fifty separate programs to aid the handicapped, most of them in HEW, and virtually all uncoordinated. Ibid., p. S 18191.

[8] Ibid., p. S 18166.

[9] Ibid., p. S 18170, statement of Senator Edmund S. Muskie (D-Me.).

[10] Ibid.

[11] Ibid. (August 2, 1978), p. S 12375, statement of Senator Percy.

[12] Ibid. (October 11, 1978), p. S 18167.

[13] Ibid. (August 3, 1978), p. H 7853.

[14] Laurence H. Silberman, "If Not the Best, At Least Not the Worst," *Common Sense,* vol. 1 (Summer 1978), pp. 18–26.

[15] These criteria are from section 4 of the Government Accountability Act.

[16] Coverage of the independent regulatory agencies was omitted in these bills because of their relatively limiting spending.

[17] Section 2(a) of the Government Accountability Act, except as found in S. 2 and H.R. 2.

[18] *Congressional Record,* vol. 124 (August 2, 1978), p. S 12374, statement of Senator Percy.

[19] Ibid. (September 7, 1978), p. E 4839, statement of Representative William A. Steiger (R-Wis.).

[20] Ibid., vol. 125 (May 16, 1979), p. E 2339, statement of Representative Erlenborn (R-Ill.).

[21] Ibid. (May 16, 1979), p. S 6089, statement of Senator Percy.

[22] Ibid.

[23] Silberman, "If Not the Best," p. 26.

[24] Ibid., p. 25.

[25] *Congressional Record,* vol. 125 (May 16, 1979), p. S 6090, statement of Senator Percy.

[26] Ibid., vol. 124 (September 7, 1978), p. E 4839, statement of Representative Steiger.

[27] George Will, "Report Cards for Federal Programs," *The Washington Post,* October 8, 1978.

[28] *Congressional Record,* vol. 124 (October 11, 1978), p. S 18168; and see Senate Report 95-326, p. 14.

[29] One columnist claims the phrase ZBB has joined other slogans in the graveyard of panaceas. Will, "Report Cards for Federal Programs."

[30] See the statements of Senator Henry Bellmon (R-Okla.) during the debate on sunset legislation, *Congressional Record,* vol. 124 (October 11, 1978), p. S 18212. Senator Percy claims the endorsement of former OMB directors George Shultz and Caspar Weinberger for the Government Accountability Act. The Committee for Economic Development contends the threat of sunsetting is too drastic to be used often. It recommends requiring agencies to submit periodic evaluations of their programs and requiring them publicly to rank major programs from least to most effective. "Regulatory Reform: Business Group Urges Tougher Evaluation, Oversight of Government Programs," *Bureau of National Affairs Daily Report for Executives,* July 25, 1979, p. A-12.

[31] U.S. Congress, Senate, Committee on Governmental Affairs, *1979 Senate Hearings on Sunset Legislation,* 96th Congress, 1st session, June 7, 1979, testimony of Bowman Cutter, executive associate director of OMB.

[32] Ibid.

[33] Ibid.

[34] See section 602 of title VI of S. 2 as it would be modified by the compromise.

[35] *1979 Senate Hearings on Sunset Legislation,* July 24, 1979, statement of Bowman Cutter.

AEI Legislative Analyses

AEI Associates Program

The American Enterprise Institute invites your participation in the competition of ideas through its AEI Associates Program. This program has two objectives:

The first is to broaden the distribution of AEI studies, conferences, forums, and reviews, and thereby to extend public familiarity with the issues. AEI Associates receive regular information on AEI research and programs, and they can order publications and cassettes at a savings.

The second objective is to increase the research activity of the American Enterprise Institute and the dissemination of its published materials to policy makers, the academic community, journalists, and others who help shape public attitudes. Your contribution, which in most cases is partly tax deductible, will help ensure that decision makers have the benefit of scholarly research on the practical options to be considered before programs are formulated. The issues studied by AEI include:

Defense Policy	Health Policy
Economic Policy	Legal Policy
Energy Policy	Political and Social Processes
Foreign Policy	Social Security and Retirement Policy
Government Regulation	Tax Policy

For more information, write to: AMERICAN ENTERPRISE INSTITUTE
1150 Seventeenth Street, N.W.
Washington, D.C. 20036

American Enterprise Institute for Public Policy Research
1150 Seventeenth Street, N.W.   Washington, D.C. 20036   (202) 862-5800